Contents

The Manager 04
We are the Champions 06
10 Key moments 16
The Players 28
The Fans 58
Attacking spearhead 62
What they said 64

 @lfc  liverpoolfc  liverpoolfc

Editor David Cottrell **Assistant Editor** William Hughes
Writer Chris McLoughlin **Production Editor** Michael McGuinness
Design Rick Cooke, James Maluchnik, Glen Hind, Lee Ashun & Colin Sumpter
Subeditors Nick Moreton & Simon Monk
Photography Press Association, Getty Images, Liverpool Echo, John Powell, Andrew Powell, Nicholas Taylor

Published by Reach Sport
Managing Director Steve Hanrahan **Commercial Director** Will Beedles
Executive Art Editor Rick Cooke **Executive Editor** Paul Dove
Marketing & Communications Manager Claire Brown
Website www.reachsportshop.com **Printed by** William Gibbons

'It's a wonderful moment'

Jürgen Klopp

"I cannot sum up my emotions because if I tried to start talking about it [how I feel] again, I will start crying again! I am completely overwhelmed; I don't know, it's a mix of everything – I am relieved, I am happy, I am proud. I couldn't be more proud of the boys. How we watched the game [Chelsea v Manchester City] together, we knew it could happen, it could not happen, we didn't know.

"We want to play football and we are really happy that we are allowed to play again – then when it happened in that moment, it was a pure explosion. When we counted down the last five seconds of the game, the ref counted down a little bit longer than us so we had to look at two or three more passes! Then it was pure... I cannot describe it. It was a really, really nice moment. Directly after it, I felt so empty inside – I cannot believe it, I am really not happy with myself in the moment that I feel like I feel, but it's just a little bit too much in the moment. I will be fine, nobody has to worry!

"I actually couldn't be happier; I couldn't have dreamed of something like that and I never did before last year, honestly. We were not close enough three years ago, a year ago we were really close... what the boys have done in the last two-and-a-half years, the consistency they show is absolutely incredible and second to none. Honestly, I have no idea how we do that all the time. Last night, a very good example – we played a game [v Crystal Palace] like the stadium is fully packed and everybody is shouting 'Liverpool' or whatever constantly. It is a wonderful moment, that's what I can say.

"Thirty years ago... I was 23, so I didn't think too much about winning a title with Liverpool, to be honest! I had no skills for that! Thirty years later I am here and because of the great staff I have, it is unbelievable. It is for everybody; they all put so much effort into it and I am the lucky guy who sits in the seat in this moment and... can be part of this story. It's so great it is unbelievable.

"The boys love being part of this club, they love being part of the story of this club and the history. It is so nice how we learned how to deal with the history, how we learned to use the history in the last two years. It is just amazing."

L.F.C.
Champions 2019/20

WE ARE THE
CHAM

2019/20

PIONS

And now you're gonna believe us... we've gone and won the league!

It has been a long, long wait but in many ways that just helps to make it taste all the sweeter.

To add context, only a handful of the Liverpool squad that has just been crowned champions, James Milner, Dejan Lovren, Adam Lallana, Adrian and Andy Lonergan were even born when the Reds last claimed the title of being the best in England.

Since Kenny Dalglish's men won the old First Division in 1990, six managers – and Sir Kenny himself – have tried to get their hands on the Premier League trophy without success.

When Jürgen Klopp was appointed manager in October 2015 he didn't say whether he had a five-year plan.

But if he did, it couldn't have been executed any better with the past year or so seeing Liverpool FC restored to their place among the elite of club football. Champions of Europe? Tick? Champions of the world? Tick. And finally, gloriously, champions of England? Tick.

There have been many highlights along the way as the Reds stormed to the title with the 24 players used before the title was clinched when Chelsea beat Manchester City all playing their part.

From some important saves made by goalkeepers Alisson Becker and Adrian to the defensive attributes of centre-backs Virgil van Dijk, Joe Gomez, Joel Matip and Dejan Lovren there has been much to admire. The energy and attacking flair of Trent Alexander-Arnold and Andy Robertson, two men who have helped redefine the role of full-back, has given the Reds an added dimension ever since they burst onto the Anfield scene.

In midfield, the counter-pressing work-rate combined with tremendous skill sets of regulars such as captain Jordan Henderson leading by example, Gini Wijnaldum, Fabinho and the effervescent Milner set the tone in so many matches and there ware also important contributions along the way from Alex Oxlade-Chamberlain and Naby Keita.

Any team in the land would love a front three of Roberto Firmino, Sadio Mane and Mohamed Salah and the trio had contributed 40 goals and 21 assists in the Premier League by the time the championship was confirmed.

Providing back-up were Divock Origi, Xherdan Shaqiri and January addition Takumi Minamino while teenagers Curtis Jones, Harvey Elliott and Neco Williams made their league debuts for the Reds during the historic season.

And moulding them all together was the dynamic leadership of Klopp and his backroom staff.

The German's impact was summed up perfectly by Alexander-Arnold, a wonderful young talent who has blossomed at first-team level since being handed his debut by the manager back in 2016.

Speaking in June, the England international said: "When you think back to where the club was when he took over to now, the things he's done for the club have been mind-blowing. To change the whole club, to change everybody from doubters to believers, just to get everyone thinking and believing in the same way and having the same dreams, he just embodies the whole club.

"I think every person who's been involved with him can only thank him as much as possible because the way he develops the people around him into making their dreams come true and helping them do the things that they want to is amazing. I think he's someone who will always be special to the club and for me personally."

KLOPP MAN: The boss has helped end a 30-year wait for the title

FROM DOUBTERS TO BELIEVERS, EVERYONE HAVING THE SAME DREAMS

Some have stated that this team is already the best in Liverpool FC's history. Quite a claim. And for that to gain credence the team will probably need to underpin this season's success with a sustained run of silverware although four trophies in just over 12 months isn't a bad start.

Aside from the incredible points tally the Reds have racked up, this triumph has highlighted the vast reserves of character and desire running through every sinew of the current crop.

Last season's experience could have had a very different effect. To have accrued 97 points and still not claimed the holy grail could have had a demoralising impact upon Klopp and his men.

But they wouldn't have that. Before the coronavirus pandemic brought a suspension to the season in mid-March, Liverpool had a 25-point advantage over Manchester City at the summit of the table, an incredible swing.

Of course, we had seen evidence of this extraordinary will to win before. In 2018, Liverpool reached the Champions League final in Kiev only to lose to Real Madrid in heartbreaking style.

But rather than be set off course by the experience, Klopp's Reds rolled up their sleeves and put it right the following season. Few then should have ever doubted that they wouldn't do the same again.

When Liverpool clinched their last league title in April 1990, Madonna topped the UK singles charts with *Vogue*. Thirty years on Liverpool FC are very much back in footballing fashion. And doesn't it feel just wonderful?

CHAMPIONS
20
Standard Chartered
LFC
Standard Chartered
CHAMPIONS
19-20

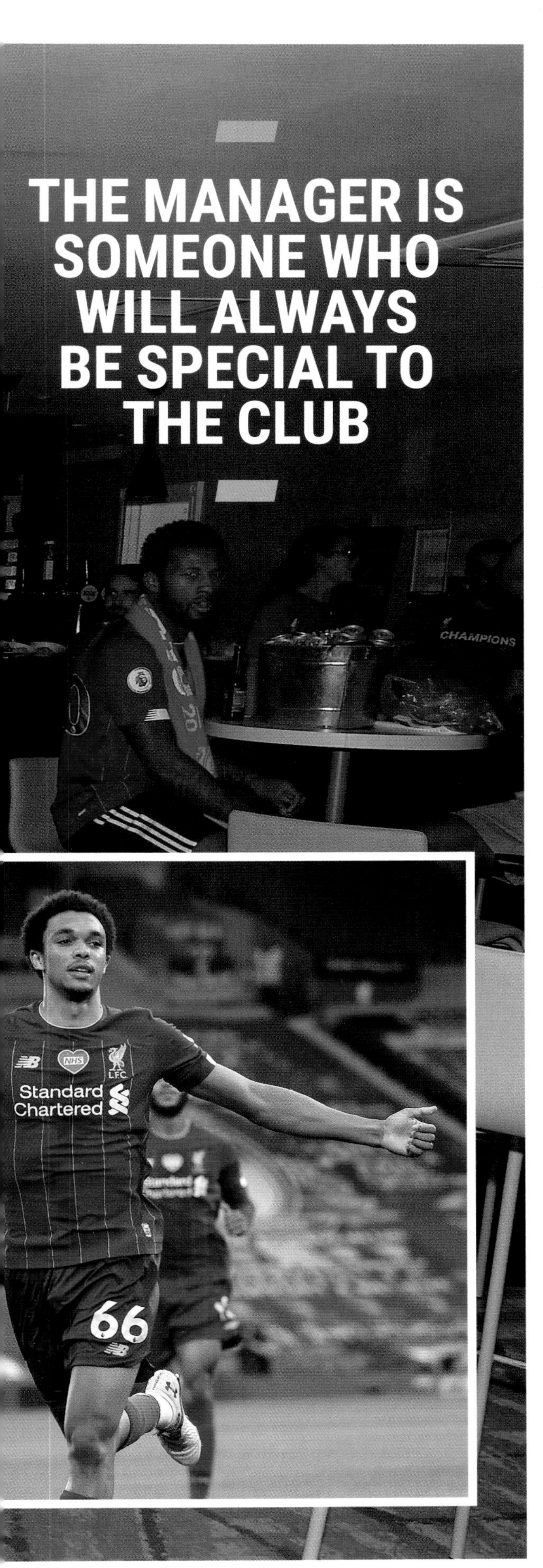

THE MANAGER IS SOMEONE WHO WILL ALWAYS BE SPECIAL TO THE CLUB

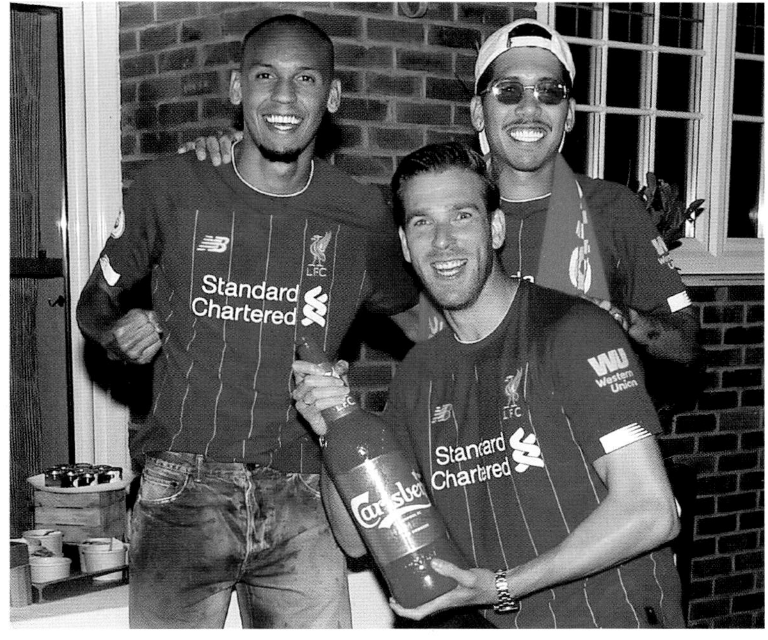

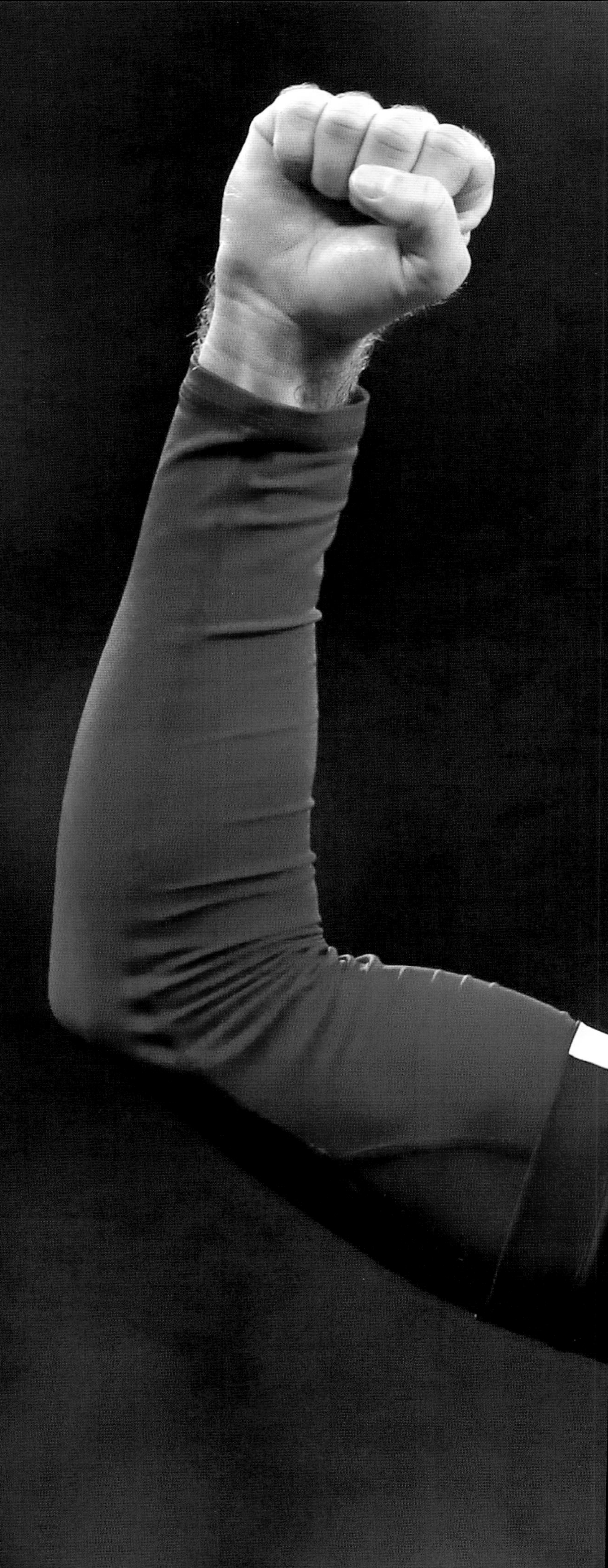

'I'm very proud'

Jordan Henderson

"I could never in words describe the feeling of winning the Premier League, just like I couldn't describe winning the Champions League. It's a unique feeling and one that, again, I'm very proud of. I've been so honoured to be part of this football club right from the first moment that I came and to go on the journey to be with this manager, this group of players, these fans – it's been so special.

"It's amazing, it's hard to describe to be honest. But after the final whistle [of the Chelsea v Manchester City game] it was just an amazing feeling again, especially to spend it with all the lads and the staff. To finally get over the line is a relief but also an amazing feeling.

"We'll enjoy this, we'll celebrate, but then I know in the next few days they'll be straight onto the next game, which is City, and finishing the season off as well as we can. We want to win every game and we want to finish off with the highest points record we can and give that everything we've got and then we'll go into next season and we'll want even more. So it's about just keeping that hunger and I've got no doubt that we've got that because we've proved that over the past couple of years. Even when we have won trophies and we have lost trophies, we've reacted in the right way so I've got no doubt that we'll react in the right way again."

MOMEN
THAT DEFINED

TS
THE
SEASON

1. Penalty points

By the time Brendan Rodgers' Leicester City arrived at Anfield in early October, Liverpool's 100 per cent start had stretched to seven Premier League matches. The Foxes had made a strong start to the campaign and the meeting of the sides produced fast, free-flowing football that was incredibly easy on the eye. Sadio Mane's first-half opener was cancelled out by a James Maddison goal with just 10 minutes remaining and the Reds looked set to drop their first points of the 2019/20. However in stoppage time, a mix-up between Leicester substitute Marc Albrighton and his goalkeeper Kasper Schmeichel saw Mane upended and referee Chris Kavanagh pointed to the penalty spot. With VAR now in full operation, a check was made and the decision upheld. The nerveless James Milner took on the duties from 12 yards and there was never really any doubt about the outcome. Anfield erupted and Liverpool had made it eight wins out of eight.

2. Inside number nine

The Reds' perfect start to the campaign eventually came to an end in game number nine at Old Trafford but a late rally saw Jürgen Klopp's men remain unbeaten. Liverpool had been baffled at the failure of VAR to overturn a seemingly clear foul by United defender Victor Lindelof on Divock Origi in the build-up to Marcus Rashford's opener for the home side. As the minutes ticked by, United dropped deeper and deeper in a bid to bolster their defensive rearguard and hold on to what they had. Liverpool's territorial dominance eventually paid dividends with five minutes left when substitute Adam Lallana was picked out by Andy Robertson's cross from the left and he calmly swept the ball beyond David De Gea.

3. City slickers

Mid-November brought the first meeting of the teams who had accumulated 195 points between them in 2018/19. The fact that City pipped Liverpool by just one – 98 to 97 - had left the Reds fired up and they produced a stunning performance to bag a 3-1 victory that saw them move nine points clear of Pep Guardiola's side and also open up an eight point advantage over Leicester and Chelsea at the top. The contest had been billed as a potentially defining moment in the season and the Reds rose to the occasion. They were ahead inside six minutes when Fabinho crashed a 25-yarder past Claudio Bravo. The advantage was doubled seven minutes later when Mo Salah headed in Andy Robertson's perfect cross from the left. City were left smarting again after the break when Sadio Mane headed in from a Jordan Henderson centre and although the visitors pulled a goal back late on through Bernardo Silva, Liverpool ran out worthy winners. "What a game," said Jürgen Klopp afterwards. "If you want to win against City you have to do something special and we had to be intense. When City started to control it more in the last 15 minutes, it was tense, but then you saw the quality and what the boys can do. The boys did 75 minutes of unbelievable stuff."

4.

Derby delight

When the team sheets arrived in the Anfield media room ahead of kick-off in the first Merseyside derby of the season, it's fair to say there were a few double-takes. With Marco Silva's Everton about to go head-to-head with the Reds, Jürgen Klopp opted to ring the changes. Adrian came in for the suspended Alisson but elsewhere there were starts for fringe men Adam Lallana and Xherdan Shaqiri while Divock Origi, so often the scourge of the Blues, receiving the nod as Mo Salah and Roberto Firmino were named on the substitutes' bench. The new faces took their chances and the Reds came firing out of the starting blocks, racing into a 2-0 lead inside 17 minutes through Origi and Shaqiri. Michael Keane pulled one back for the Blues but Origi extended the two-goal lead which became 4-2 at the interval after Sadio Mane and Richarlison traded goals. Gini Wijnaldum added a fifth goal in front of the Kop late on as the Reds ran out worthy winners to take another important step in their quest for the title.

5.

A boss deal

Liverpool supporters were given the perfect early Christmas present in December as Friday the 13th proved to be a lucky day. That was when the club announced that Jürgen Klopp and his assistant managers Peter Krawietz and Pep Lijnders had agreed contract extensions with the Reds. The deals extended the time 'the normal one' and his backroom team will stay at Anfield until 2024 and gave all Reds a big boost ahead of a heavy Christmas and early new year schedule. "For me personally this is a statement of intent, one which is built on my knowledge of what we as a partnership have achieved so far and what is still there for us to achieve," he explained. "When I see the development of the club and the collaborative work that continues to take place, I feel my contribution can only grow. People see what happens on the pitch as a measure of our progress and although it is the best measure, it's not the only measure. I have seen the commitment from ownership through to every aspect and function of the club you can think of. This club is in such a good place, I couldn't contemplate leaving."

6.

Boxing clever

After winning the FIFA Club World Cup for the first time in Qatar, the Reds' first game back on English soil was their Boxing Day fixture at Leicester City. Brendan Rodgers' men had continued their fine start to the campaign and the meeting of the Premier League's top two was billed as a real test for the Reds. How would they react after flying back almost 3,500 miles? Would they be tired? Would they struggle to adapt to the change of climate? Could Leicester capitalise and reduce Liverpool's lead at the top of the table to seven points? Klopp's men provided all the answers with a devastating display as they swept aside Leicester's fantastic Mr Foxes with a 4-0 victory at the King Power. Right-back Trent Alexander-Arnold produced a standout showing with a goal and two assists, his goal rounding things off after a brace from Roberto Firmino and a penalty by James Milner had put Liverpool in full control.

7.

Go Ali go, go, go!

One of the defining moments of the campaign ended in Alisson Becker sprinting out of his penalty area towards the Kop to celebrate a goal with Mohamed Salah. The Reds were leading Manchester United 1-0 at Anfield and it was deep into stoppage time when he claimed a mis-hit shot from United's Aaron Wan-Bissaka. The goalkeeper's forward-thinking saw him play a pinpoint pass towards Mohamed Salah on the halfway line. The Egyptian then did what he does best to end the contest in front of a buoyant Kop. Alisson raced upfield in pursuit of his team-mate to celebrate!

"I could feel my legs afterwards - it was a tough race to run!" he said. "I did not plan the celebration, it was just something from the moment. Giving the assist to Mo is something that we try a lot in training. We tried it before when we played together at Roma but it [a goal] didn't happen. Then we tried it here and it happened at Anfield in a special game, in a derby against Man United. It was the last minute of the game, the match was closed and I just wanted to celebrate with the boys because I always celebrate by myself!"

8. Capital gains

The final Wednesday in January saw Liverpool visit W... United in a game originally postponed in December due t... the Reds' participation in the FIFA Club World Cup. The tea... produced another solid performance to win 2-0 thanks to a Mo Salah penalty and a fine strike from Alex Oxlade-Chamberlain. It extended Liverpool's lead at the top of the table to 19 points over Manchester City. It also meant that the Reds had beaten every other team in the Premier League since the start of the campaign, an astonishing feat to have recorded after just 24 games. "They're as good as there's been around," said West Ham manager David Moyes afterwards. "It's very difficult to say that when you've been manager of Everton and Manchester United but Liverpool are an excellent side." The triumph made it 23 wins out of those 24 matches and took the club's points tally to 70 but Jürgen Klopp was quick to play it down. "Yes we have 70 points, an incredible number, but so many things can happen. I'm not too concerned about records. We had a record at [Borussia] Dortmund and Bayern [Munich] beat it the next season. We don't feel as though anything is done, I promise you."

9. Milner marvel

The first full weekend of March saw a couple of significant results as the Reds took another huge step towards ending their wait of three decades for a top-flight title. On the Saturday lunchtime Liverpool came from behind to defeat Bournemouth 2-1 at Anfield and just over 24 hours later Manchester City lost 2-0 to Manchester United at Old Trafford. Those results gave the Reds a 25-point advantage and left them just two wins away from claiming the title. Goals from Mo Salah and Sadio Mane took the duo's combined league tally to 30 but the Reds owed a huge debt of gratitude to stand-in skipper James Milner for a late goalline clearance which kept their lead intact. Bournemouth winger Ryan Fraser clipped the ball over Adrian and towards a gaping goal but Milner, playing at left-back, read the situation perfectly and managed to sprint back before executing his last-ditch clearance to perfection by hooking the ball to safety in the nick of time. Speaking after the game, manager Jürgen Klopp outlined Milner's value to the squad. "Why would we extend his contract if he's not incredibly important to everything that we do? He wouldn't like it if we spoke just about what he's doing off the pitch and he showed why he's so important on it. That's Millie."

10. Crystal clear

The Reds' first fixture at Anfield in 110 days saw them face Crystal Palace in late June. There was a strange atmosphere with no fans allowed inside the stadium as the nation took slow steps back to normality following the coronavirus pandemic. However, Liverpool meant business from the start. Despite lacking their usual backing, the Reds simply steamrollered Palace with a typically relentless display. Afterwards LFC alumni Graeme Souness and John Barnes, serial winners during their illustrious spells at Anfield, described the performance as 'sensational'.

Trent Alexander-Arnold chose the perfect time to score his first goal of the season in L4, curling home a wonderful free-kick to calm any nerves and provide the perfect platform for victory. Fabinho then helped the Reds double their advantage on the stroke of half-time, picking out Mo Salah's incisive run behind left-back Patrick van Aanholt and allowing the Egyptian to slot in his 17th league goal of the campaign. Fabinho himself effectively made the game safe early in the second-half when he found space outside the Palace box and let rip with an absolute screamer that flew into the top corner of the Kop net. Sadio Mane then put the seal on the dynamic display by finishing off a wonderful counter-attacking passage of play which involved all of the Reds' revered front three.

It was only a shame that there were not 53,000 supporters inside the famous ground to enjoy the show, but you can be sure that many more around the globe were glued to their TV sets and toasting a victory which put their favourite team within touching distance of the trophy.

"Tonight was a big step, that's clear," said Klopp afterwards. "If we play like this, it's really not nice to play against us."

Liverpool's 23rd successive home league win had put them 23 points clear at the top of the table and it was quite apparent that Liverpool's long journey towards this particular piece of silverware was reaching a conclusion.

"The red ribbons are coming out," said Sky Sports presenter David Jones. Indeed. Liverpool's first Premier League title was confirmed 24 hours later when Manchester City dropped points at Chelsea. Boom!

EST·1892
GOMEZ
12

Standard Chartered
SALAH
11
MANÉ
10

'We feel it's our time'

Mo Salah

"I feel great. Since I came here I said I want to win the Premier League with the team. The city didn't win it for a long time, so it was the right time. Maybe last year we had a chance to win it but Man City also performed really good and they won it. I think all the players are motivated, everyone is motivated in his way – but everyone is motivated to win the league. It's our time to win it and it's great."

ALISSON BECKER

Alisson, Alisson, Alisson!

The Brazilian no1 ended his debut season at Anfield as a European champion and he now ends his second with the Reds as a world and Premier League champ too.

As well as producing his trademark string of stunning saves throughout the campaign, he is up there in the running to retain his Golden Gloves award with 12 clean sheets despite missing nine of the first 29 games through injury. In December he became the first winner of the Yashin Trophy for the best men's goalkeeper in world football. One of the enduring moments of his season will be his late assist for Mo Salah that clinched victory over Manchester United at Anfield in January, a sequence that culminated with him sprinting towards the Kop to celebrate with the Egyptian striker and their team-mates. Manager Jürgen Klopp hailed his keeper for "making the difficult things look easy," while team-mate and fellow member of the goalkeepers' union Adrian added: "I'd say that Ali is a complete goalkeeper. He is very good with his feet and he has that calmness that goalkeepers need. He's physically strong and powerful, he's quick, he re-adjusts and gets back in position really well."

L.F.C.
Standard Chartered
Western Union
AB1

Watch him defend and we watch him score

The imperious Dutchman has enjoyed another superb season at the heart of the Reds defence.

He has played every single minute of the Reds' Premier League season, an outstanding achievement for an outfield player. Often described as 'a Rolls Royce' of a defender, he makes the game look easy and has been a calming influence in the backline. As well as his commanding defending, the no4 also contributed four headed goals, all at Anfield.

There was the opening night goal against Norwich City from a Mo Salah corner, a couple of first-half efforts in the 2-1 win over Brighton in November and the hugely popular opener against Manchester United in January. He says that the experience of winning the Champions League last season made him eager to earn more silverware with the Reds.

"It makes you very hungry. Talking personally, if you experience those kind of evenings and celebrations, you want to experience it at least once a year if not a couple of times.

"So we wanted to just go for it. We have the quality in the team and we have so much potential as well so we tried to do our best to give everything we have and see where it would lead us."

VIRGIL VAN DIJK

VIRGIL
4
Josip

JOE GOMEZ

Ain't nobody like Joe Gomez

The 23-year-old started the season alongside Virgil van Dijk against Norwich City and has really come of age throughout the campaign. His pace, reading of the game and ability on the ball have all been utilised during a season that saw him pass a century of appearances for the Reds.

The England international has started more than half of the team's games and demonstrated his versatility by playing at right-back in the 3-0 win at Bournemouth in December. "The gaffer emphasises how important it is that everyone's ready and that the whole squad contributes," he told the official matchday programme in February.

"Obviously as a backline and Ali, we thrive off clean sheets but it is a collective thing. It starts from the front and works its way back. We take pride in it but we know that it's as a team that we defend and the whole team does that because it gives us a foundation to get goals. And if you get the goals and keep clean sheets, you win games."

DEJAN **LOVREN**

The centre-back started nine times alongside Virgil van Dijk before the Reds wrapped up the title and his experience was always important.

He proved he could contribute at the other end of the pitch too, producing a raking pass to Divock Origi during December's Merseyside derby at Anfield which finished with the Belgian lifting a brilliant effort over goalkeeper Jordan Pickford for Liverpool's third goal of the night. Speaking in October, he told the club's official matchday programme: "When we look at the competitions that we have there are so many games to play and so we know that we need all the squad to be ready to come in and compete when needed."

JOEL MATIP

After scoring in the FA Community Shield against Manchester City at Wembley, the central defender had his season disrupted by injuries but still played his part whenever called upon.

He made eight appearances in the Premier League by the end of March with his trademark calmness to the fore. His efforts were rewarded with a new long-term contract in October. "Joel's journey at Liverpool is one I love and I am absolutely delighted he has shown his commitment to us by signing this new long-term contract," said Jürgen Klopp. "As the team has evolved and become better, so too has Joel."

He scored his first Kop end goal in the 3-1 win over Arsenal back in August.

TRENT
ALEXANDER-

ARNOLD

The Scouser in our team

Given what he has achieved in his fledgling career to date, it's hard to believe that Trent is still only 21.

The 2019/20 season has seen him continue to grow and his value to Jürgen Klopp was demonstrated by the fact he featured in all of the Reds' first 31 games.

His quality from set-plays saw him enhance his reputation as one of the team's key attackers from his right-back station. He matched his 2018/19 record tally of a dozen PL assists with another 12 following a couple in the 3-2 defeat of West Ham at Anfield in March. He had reserved his goalscoring for key matches on the road, netting an absolute screamer from a well-worked free-kick in the 2-1 win over Chelsea at Stamford Bridge and a low arrowed drive in the 4-0 Boxing Day victory at Leicester City. He then converted a wonderful free-kick in the behind closed doors win over Crystal Palace at Anfield in June.

"For me, it's always good to be involved in the goals but the foundation of a win is always the clean sheet," he says. "It's good to contribute at both ends and when you've got the quality of players that we do, it's easier – you can put it into areas and know that the lads are going to go and attack it."

ANDY

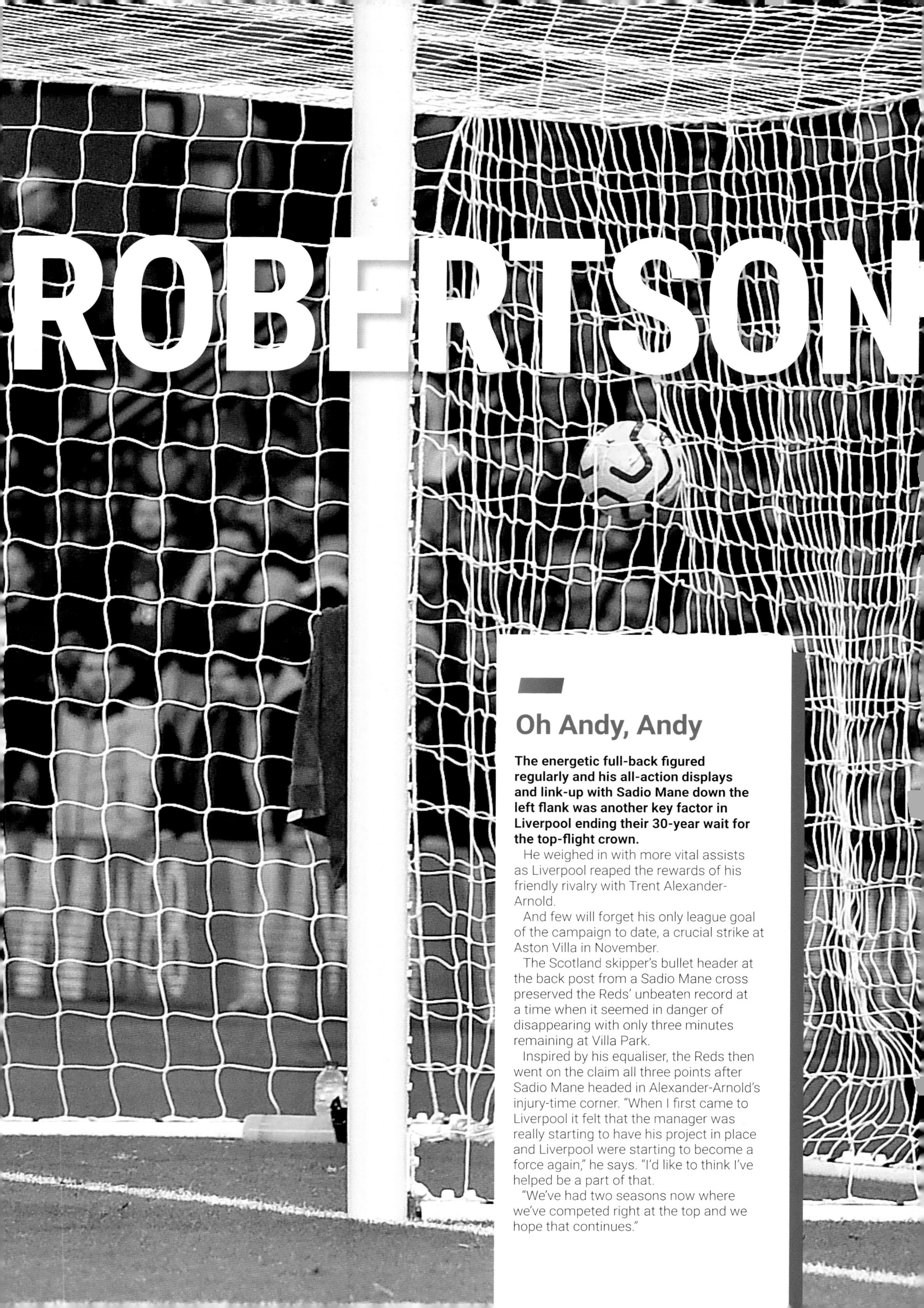

ROBERTSON

Oh Andy, Andy

The energetic full-back figured regularly and his all-action displays and link-up with Sadio Mane down the left flank was another key factor in Liverpool ending their 30-year wait for the top-flight crown.

He weighed in with more vital assists as Liverpool reaped the rewards of his friendly rivalry with Trent Alexander-Arnold.

And few will forget his only league goal of the campaign to date, a crucial strike at Aston Villa in November.

The Scotland skipper's bullet header at the back post from a Sadio Mane cross preserved the Reds' unbeaten record at a time when it seemed in danger of disappearing with only three minutes remaining at Villa Park.

Inspired by his equaliser, the Reds then went on the claim all three points after Sadio Mane headed in Alexander-Arnold's injury-time corner. "When I first came to Liverpool it felt that the manager was really starting to have his project in place and Liverpool were starting to become a force again," he says. "I'd like to think I've helped be a part of that.

"We've had two seasons now where we've competed right at the top and we hope that continues."

JORDAN

Here's to you, Jordan Henderson

The leading man, Hendo has been an important figure in the team's success, driving them on to further success on the back of lifting the Champions League, UEFA Super Cup and FIFA Club World Cup trophies.

Highly valued by his team-mates and Kopites, the long-serving Red has been a vital component in one of the hardest-working midfields in the global game. Personal highlights included goals in the home wins over Tottenham Hotspur and Southampton as well as one in the 2-1 victory at Wolves.

He also produced five assists, with his key contributions in the home win over Manchester City in November and the pass for Sadio Mane's winning goal at Norwich City in February.

Henderson has continually impressed on the team the 'game-by-game' mentality which served them so well. "Throughout the season we've collectively blocked any acclaim out and focused on our jobs at hand," he said in his matchday programme notes for the Bournemouth game in March. "Part of that process is remembering our qualities and not being distracted by the noise outside.

"The reason why we have been so strong in the Premier League is because it is what our performances since the start of the season have deserved."

Chartered

Der, der, der der, der, der, Gini Wijnaldum!

A model of consistency in the Reds midfield, Gini is another whose value to the team can be gauged by the number of times his manager selects him.

The Dutchman played in all but one of the Reds' first 29 games of the campaign and he covered many a mile as he offered protection to the defence and support to the attack throughout the course of his all-action displays.

He also popped up with three vital goals. The only one of the game against Sheffield United at Bramall Lane in September was important in keeping the Reds' winning momentum going, while he also enjoyed his first Merseyside derby goal in the 5-2 defeat of Everton at Anfield in December.

The no5 also put the Reds on their way to a hard-fought victory against West Ham United in February, opening the scoring with a ninth-minute header.

"If you go back a few years ago, we made mistakes," he said. "But we learned from the mistakes we made and I think that's why we have been so good. We have worked really hard for that, to have it the way it is right now."

GINI WIJNALDUM

JAMES MILNER

There's only one James Milner...

Mr Reliable and a big voice in the dressing room. As well as playing with distinction in numerous positions, his leadership skills have been on display throughout.

This was particularly evident ahead of the game against Bournemouth at Anfield in March. Wearing the armband in place of the injured Jordan Henderson, he was captured by TV cameras during the pre-match warm-up reminding his fellow Reds of the standards demanded of them.

He backed up his words with actions, producing a breathtaking goal-line clearance to keep the Reds' lead intact late on in the game as the team secured a 2-1 win which, by the end of that weekend, would take them to within two victories of claiming the league title.

At the other end of the field, his nerves of steel were on display as he converted penalties in both games against Leicester City, particularly in the Anfield meeting in October when he dispatched an injury-time spot-kick to secure a 2-1 success.

Manager Jürgen Klopp said of the 34-year-old: "Exceptional, exceptional. It just sets the benchmark, that you're 33/34 and doing things like he is. Obviously age is no issue. That's why he has [played] like 7,680 Premier League games!"

FABINHO

The defensive midfielder has made a huge impact in his two seasons since making the move from Monaco and was a key figure in the centre of the park.

The Brazilian contributed a brilliant long-range goal in the defining 3-1 win against Manchester City at Anfield, a victory that added to the belief in the dressing-room that this could be the Reds' season. He thumped in a similar strike in the 4-0 win over Crystal Palace in June that put the Reds within touching distance of the title.

He was nicknamed 'Dyson' by Jürgen Klopp for the impressive way he vacuums up danger in front of the Reds' back four following the 2-1 win over Tottenham Hotspur at Anfield in October.

"A few people call me this!" he revealed. "Between us players I'm more known as Flaco (the skinny one), but they're cool nicknames. Before the coach used it [Dyson], another player used it — I think [James] Milner might have said it.

"It's a cool nickname, but the other one that the majority of the players use, Flaco, was started by Virgil [van Dijk] and everybody started calling me it."

ALEX OXLADE-CHAMBERLAIN

Having had to sit out most of the 2018/19 season through injury, it was a huge boost for the Reds to be able to call upon the England international throughout this campaign.

A dynamic player with the ability to drive at defenders from a midfield berth, he has netted three important goals throughout the title-winning campaign.

His first league strike of the season came in the 3-0 win at Bournemouth in December and he later scored in successive games in victories at West Ham United and at home to Southampton.

"There are crucial players in the team who, if we only come off the pitch with a draw instead of a win, aren't happy," he told the official matchday programme in January. "That's the environment we've created.

"In the past I've been in teams where, if we didn't have our best technical game, or the football wasn't that good, we wouldn't come away with a win. With this team we manage to grind out wins in those moments.

"That's nothing but mentality and sticking to the basics when the nice stuff isn't coming off or individuals aren't doing some of the amazing things that they can do. That's the difference that keeps us going."

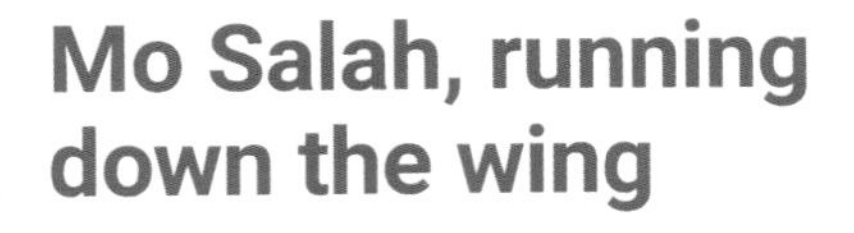

Mo Salah, running down the wing

Another stellar season for the Egyptian King as he became the first Liverpool player since Michael Owen to score 20 goals in three successive seasons.

His strike in the 2-1 win over Bournemouth in March also saw him mark his 100th Premier League outing for the Reds with his 70th goal – a tally bettered by nobody in the club's proud 128-year history.

After finishing fourth in the Ballon d'Or in December, he went on to fire the Reds to their first top-flight title in 30 years with his finish against Crystal Palace post-restart his 17th goal in Premier League action.

He needed just 19 minutes to open his account for the campaign in the 4-1 defeat of Norwich City on the opening night and went on to net braces in the home wins over Arsenal, Watford and Southampton. Other highlights included his first goal against Manchester United in the 2-0 win over the Red Devils at Anfield in January.

After the game against Bournemouth, Jürgen Klopp said: "He is an outstanding striker, a world-class striker. It's really nice, I'm really happy for him that he reached that mark [20 goals]. We need the boys because with all the good stuff you can do on the pitch, in the end you need somebody to finish it off and very often, thank God, it is Mo."

MOHAMED SALAH

L.F.C.
Standard Chartered
WU
Western Union
11

Standard
Chartered
LFC
L.F.C

Hear the Kopites sing, Mane!

The Senegalese attacker enjoyed a standout season as he helped the Reds claim their fourth major trophy in less than 12 months.

With his combination of pace and power, he was a constant handful for defenders, most of whom found him simply too hot to handle. His superb form saw him pip team-mate Mo Salah to be named African Player of the Year for 2019.

Sadio had scored 15 times in the Premier League action following his goal in the 4-0 defeat of Crystal Palace in June. His tally included a spectacular double against Newcastle in September, a last-gasp winner at Aston Villa in November and a strike from outside the box in the Merseyside derby at Anfield in December.

As well as those decisive goals against Villa and Bournemouth, he also contributed match-winning strikes against Wolves and West Ham in front of the Kop and at Norwich City.

And that goal against Palace, in the first game at Anfield following Project Restart, set the seal on a victory that put the Reds within two points of making the championship a mathematical certainty.

"I always say it is very easy to work together," he told Liverpool FC's official club magazine of his link-up with Firmino and Salah. "Personally I just think myself very lucky to play alongside these great players. Everybody who plays alongside them would enjoy it because they make everything easy, so I just enjoy playing alongside them.

"We are all from different countries and speak different first languages but I think football is one language and it is universal so everybody can speak it. It is the same with Mo, Bobby and myself."

SADIO MANE

ROBERTO

The best in the world is Bobby Firmino

It was one of those strange quirks of fate that Liverpool's no9 was somehow unable to put his name on the scoresheet in home league games before the title was wrapped up.

On the road however, it was very much a case of 'give the ball to Bobby and he will score' with eight vital strikes away from Anfield.

Before 2019 was out, he netted what proved to be the Reds' important second goal in 2-1 victories at Southampton in August and Chelsea in October, a late winner at Selhurst Park against Crystal Palace in November and a brace in the brilliant 4-0 win at Leicester City on Boxing Day.

Into 2020 the Brazilian, fresh from scoring vital goals in the Reds' Club World Championship triumph in Qatar, was on target again in January with the only goal of the game on Liverpool's first trip to the Tottenham Hotspur Stadium and a late winner on a Thursday night visit to Wolves. With eight assists to complement his usual selfless displays, he remained a vital part of Jürgen Klopp's line-up. "Bobby - what can I say about him that not everybody knows already?" the boss said in September. "He's an incredibly important player.

"He enjoys it so much to play in this team, to be really there with all these super guys around him. That's what helps him then, of course: if you have the speed around you, you can be this little cheeky guy in between the lines, being there and scoring the goals. Yeah, he's a very valuable player for us."

FIRMINO

ADRIAN

The Spaniard won the first major honour of his career when he became Liverpool's penalty shoot-out hero in Istanbul as the team won the European Super Cup.

A free transfer signing last summer, the former West Ham man has proven to be an able deputy for Alisson whenever called upon and has made some important saves for the Reds on their way to the title, such as a vital stop from England striker Tammy Abraham in the 2-1 win over Chelsea at Stamford Bridge back in September. "As soon as I signed for Liverpool I just wanted to do whatever I could to help my team-mates and help the team," he explained.

"I always knew Liverpool was a big club but when you are inside the training pitch, inside the stadium and inside the dressing room with the players, the staff and the technical staff you can truly see the dimensions that the club has. It's so, so big but the other part of it is that it is still like a family. The club wants everyone to be altogether and they are big on caring about the small details. I think that is the right way to be in order to keep improving."

ADAM LALLANA

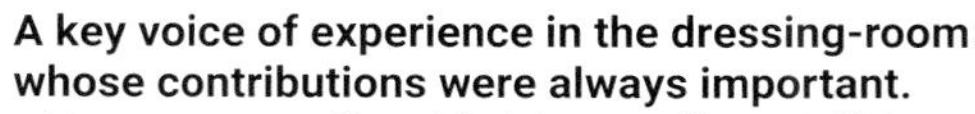

A key voice of experience in the dressing-room whose contributions were always important.

None more so than his late equaliser at Old Trafford when the Reds' unbeaten start seemed to be under threat before he popped up to convert Andy Robertson's inviting cross with five minutes remaining. He started three times with Liverpool winning all three: away to Aston Villa and at home to Everton and Wolves. Away from league action, he also led by example as a young Liverpool side defeated Everton at Anfield for the second time in a month, this time in the FA Cup third round.

DIVOCK **ORIGI**

Mostly used as a substitute, the big Belgian played his part whenever called upon and was always an added goalscoring threat for Jürgen Klopp to summon.

He scored on the opening day of the season as the Reds started as they meant to go on with a 4-1 win over Norwich City on a wet Friday night at Anfield. Another highlight was the Merseyside derby against Everton in December. Handed another start, he scored two first-half goals as the Reds went on to brush the Blues aside 5-2. Despite only starting a handful of times he also contributed a couple of assists.

"I'm fully focused with all my energy to help the team," he said in March. "Sometimes it means starting the game, sometimes coming on later. I see us as a unit. Every game, the coach has to make decisions, so for me it's important that the team always comes first. Many people speculate but I have learnt not to waste energy on this kind of thing."

XHERDAN **SHAQIRI**

It was a frustrating campaign for the Swiss attacker but there was a personal highlight.

Handed one of only two starts in his league campaign in the Merseyside derby at Anfield in December, he made his mark by scoring at the Anfield Road end after getting on the end of Sadio Mane's clever pass.

NABY **KEITA**

The Guinean's appearances were limited but, when available, he was always a handy ace up Jürgen Klopp's sleeve.

His best day came at Bournemouth's Vitality Stadium in December when he played a starring role in the Reds' 3-0 win over Eddie Howe's men. Naby scored to give Liverpool a two-goal advantage on the stroke of half-time and then turned provider after the break, teeing up Mo Salah for the Reds' third. Talking of his injury problems, he said: "In football there are difficult moments, but you mustn't drop your shoulders, you need to carry on working and that's how you win."

TAKUMI **MINAMINO**

The Japanese international was brought in during the January transfer window after impressing for FC Salzburg in their two Champions League games against the Reds during the autumn, scoring in the 4-3 thriller at Anfield in October.

He was used sparingly as he acclimatised to the Premier League but had his first taste of England's top league coming off the bench against Wolves, Southampton and Watford and made his first start at Everton in June.

NECO WILLIAMS

The 19-year-old Welshman made history in June when he became the first player in the club's history to make his league debut in a behind closed doors fixture at Anfield.

The right-back made an impact during his brief substitute appearance too, having two shots at the Crystal Palace goal and forcing his compatriot Wayne Hennessey into one excellent save. Earlier in the season, Neco had featured in the Reds' Carabao and FA Cup campaigns.

HARVEY ELLIOTT

The 16-year-old became the second youngest player to represent the Reds in league action (after Jack Robinson) when he came off the bench in the 2-0 win over Sheffield United in the Reds' first match of 2020.

The precociously talented teenager had been one of four signings Liverpool had made during the summer when he was recruited from Fulham and he also made contributions in the team's FA Cup and Carabao Cup campaigns.

CURTIS JONES

After scoring the winning penalty in front of the Kop in a thrilling Carabao Cup tie against Arsenal which had ended in an unlikely 5-5 draw, the gifted teenage midfielder made his Premier League debut in the 3-0 win at Bournemouth in December, coming on as a replacement for Andy Robertson.

He had scored a brilliant winner against Everton in the FA Cup third round before he made his second league appearance, again coming off the bench in an away win, this time at West Ham United in late January.

THE FANS

Liverpool's Twelfth Man have been the special ingredient in the Reds' title-winning recipe...

Anfield has roared on Jürgen Klopp's men every step of the way. With average attendances north of 53,000 following the redevelopment of the Main Stand four seasons ago, the Reds' famous home played a huge part in the club's 19th championship triumph.

The Kop chorus provided a noisy soundtrack to the march to glory as the team eclipsed their best-ever winning league sequence on home soil of 21 games, set by Bill Shankly's side in 1972 and early 1973. The 2-1 victory over Bournemouth in March made it 22 successive home league successes at Anfield, a run dating back to a 3-0 defeat of the Cherries back on 9 February 2019.

The volume went up a notch or two for games against key rivals. The midweek Merseyside derby against Everton was one case in point while Anfield also brought its Sunday best for the victories against the Manchester clubs.

The decibel count was up there with any European night when the stadium reacted to the second goal against United in January – Mo Salah's strike that sealed a 2-0 victory.

Jürgen Klopp might not have been too comfortable with it, but in the aftermath of Salah's strike, the Kop broke their silence on the team's title credentials. "And now you're gonna believe us...we're gonna win the league,' they bellowed. At the time, the Reds had moved 16 points clear of Pep Guardiola's Manchester City after 22 matches with a game in hand.

Afterwards, central defender Joe Gomez said: "It can't be underestimated how big the fans are for us in making the atmosphere at Anfield what it is.

"It's massive in the way that they get behind the team. It gives us such strength and that drive to perform and run those extra yards."

As Gomez and his team-mates closed in on the title, the support again came to the fore to help them come from behind to defeat Bournemouth 2-1. It was a result that took the Reds to within three victories of clinching the title. Barely 24 hours later, following Manchester United's defeat of Manchester City at Old Trafford, the tally required was just two wins.

After that match, manager Jürgen Klopp said: "[We have] a wonderful stadium with a sensational crowd. I

“IT CAN’T BE UNDERESTIMATED HOW BIG THE FANS ARE FOR US IN MAKING THE ATMOSPHERE AT ANFIELD WHAT IT IS”

think that was the best 12.30 [kick-off] performance of our crowd since I was here. I loved it.”

Skipper Jordan Henderson was injured for that fixture but in his programme notes for the Reds’ next match, the Champions League round of 16 clash with Atletico Madrid, he too referenced the special atmosphere.

“Being a supporter on Saturday, I made a point of properly soaking in the feeling around Anfield in those final few minutes and seconds and in particular what was happening on the Kop. It made me realise why it’s so important.

“It was genuinely incredible to look at with all the colours and flags and the noise was unreal. It looked and sounded amazing.

“I’ve mentioned Spion Kop 1906 in these notes previously, but the work they do and the effort they put in is always worth highlighting because it makes such a positive impact. They, more than anyone, are responsible for making the feeling so raw and authentic.

“I saw on social media that they had 50 new flags made for the Bournemouth game and, from a player’s point-of-view, the Kop looked better than ever. I don’t know if you’ve noticed, but if you watch our players just before we assemble for kick-off, most have a proper look at the Kop and try to take a moment to take it all in.

“Part of having something special in life is making sure you never take it for granted. That counts for so many things – but as a Liverpool player the positive impact of Anfield and the Kop should be top of that list.”

Of course it was a huge shame that fans couldn’t be present inside Anfield for the final four home games of the season following the coronavirus pandemic.

So many supporters had dreamed of seeing the Reds lift the Premier League trophy in front of the Kop and that will have to wait. For now.

Nonetheless, the joy of watching Liverpool crowned champions of England again, however remotely, was a sight to behold for every Red.

Speaking before the first of Liverpool’s behind closed doors at Anfield, Virgil van Dijk told the official matchday programme: “The supporters not being there will be so strange. Particularly as our supporters are so important to us. But, like so much in this time, we have to make the best of it.

“The supporters haven’t disappeared, they will just be somewhere else. We know we will have millions of people watching us from their homes so we still have the responsibility to perform for them and ourselves.

“The whole world has had to make sacrifices in the last three months or more and unfortunately the way things are at the moment means we play at the stadium and the supporters watch from their homes. But we have a strong enough connection to our fans to know they’ll be with us for every kick, header, pass, shot and save.

“It’s not that Liverpool fans aren’t around anymore – they just have to watch from home. I think we can still make this cool if we all really give our best. We’ll do that as players.

“The supporters know we feel them still. I really hope we can help bring some joy with what we do on the pitch. That will be a motivation for us.”

ENDERSON
14
verpoolfc.com/

YNWA
WE ARE ONE TEAM
THE KOP SPIRIT SURVIVES
BILL'S LEGACY LIVES ON
Premier League
MATCHCENTRE.LIVERPOOLFC.COM
The Unbearables
LIVERPOOL
LIVERPOOL F.C.
SUPPORT & BELIEVE
FOLLOW AT HOME
EXIT 204
EXIT 203
EXIT 202
EXIT 103

TOP SCORER

Just go with the Mo

Spearheading the Reds' route to glory was the indefatigable Mohamed Salah.

At the time the title was clinched the Egyptian was the Reds' leading marksman just as he has been in each of his previous two campaigns with Liverpool FC. With seven games to go, Mo had scored 17 times in the Premier League. Many of them were goals from the top drawer with this early-season effort against Arsenal typical of his repertoire. Receiving the ball on the right just inside the Gunners' half he used his skills to nick the ball away from defender David Luiz and then use his blistering pace to run free of the Brazilian and the covering Nacho Monreal before cutting inside and calmly slotting a low finish across keeper Bernd Leno and into the net at the Anfield Road end.

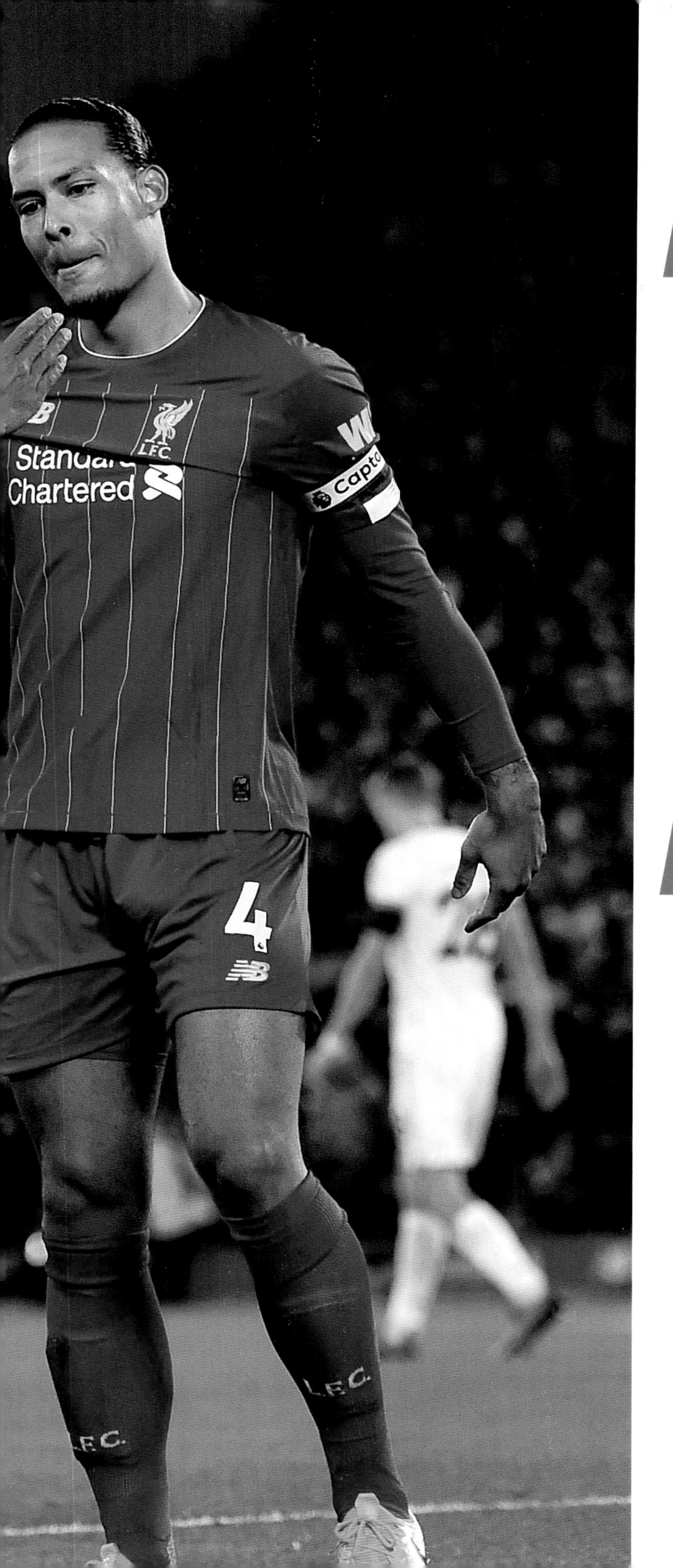

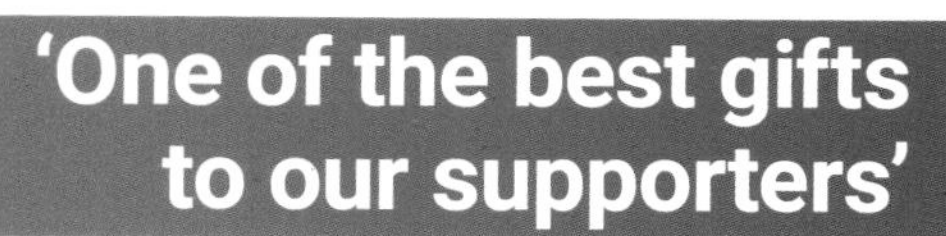

'One of the best gifts to our supporters'

Gini Wijnaldum

"It's difficult to describe but I can say that I'm really happy and really pleased that I can be a part of this team, be a part of this club. And I'm really happy that this time we can give this title to the supporters because they have waited so long for this title. The supporters were so loyal during the years since I'm here and even before I came here. That makes it more beautiful because when you have such loyal supporters and you can give them one of the best gifts, it makes it more beautiful."

'This group of players are special'

Virgil van Dijk

"I didn't have the time really to sit down and think about what happened over the last two-and-a-half seasons. I'm sure that time will come and if I'm thinking about it right now, it's just incredible. It's obviously something that every player hopes for if they make a step to a different club, to be achieving great things and proving doubters wrong and with this group of players we just enjoy the game as well. It's just fantastic to see the work we put in day in, day out and the work we want to put in as well. Everyone wants to achieve great things. Obviously there is always room for improvement but this group of players are special and I am just very proud to be part of it."

'Something we've always dreamed of'

Trent Alexander-Arnold

"We probably thought as a team we would be able to do it ourselves, but we don't really care how we did it at the end of the day. We are Premier League champions and we are proud of that. Obviously things are not as we imagined probably a few months ago or even a year ago how we imagined to win the Premier League, but we are not going to complain and make a fuss of. It's something we've always dreamed of. As fans I think it's something that will always be remembered."

'We've always been hungry to win trophies for this club'

Andy Robertson

"As a squad we're so close. We love coming in to training every single day. If somebody is having a bad game, we dig them out of a hole and we stick together on the pitch, we stick together off the pitch – that's why this squad is so special. I love being a part of it. We're all kind of brothers and we have a dad figure in the gaffer and he's the one that leads us in the right direction. Him and his staff have been second to none, to be fair, since I've came here. This season they've been excellent to us going, keep us hungry, keep us motivated. Motivation has never been a struggle. As players we've always been hungry and we always wanted to win trophies for this club. Luckily, we're now showing that in the last 12 months."